Gay Questions

Quizzical Queries Into How You Think, Feel, Love, & Live

Gay Questions

REVISED AND EXPANDED

Jerry Holderman

alyson books

LOS ANGELES • NEW YORK

© 1997, 1998 BY JERRY HOLDERMAN. ALL RIGHTS RESERVED.
COVER PHOTOGRAPH BY ROBERT SEBREE.

MANUFACTURED IN THE UNITED STATES OF AMERICA.
PRINTED ON ACID-FREE PAPER.

THIS TRADE PAPERBACK ORIGINAL IS PUBLISHED BY
ALYSON PUBLICATIONS INC.,
P.O. BOX 4371, LOS ANGELES, CALIFORNIA 90078-4371.
DISTRIBUTION IN THE UNITED KINGDOM BY
TURNAROUND PUBLISHER SERVICES LTD.,
UNIT 3 OLYMPIA TRADING ESTATE, COBURG ROAD, WOOD GREEN,
LONDON N22 6TZ ENGLAND.

FIRST EDITION: NOVEMBER 1997
SECOND EDITION: SEPTEMBER 1998

02 01 00 99 98   10 9 8 7 6 5 4 3 2 1

ISBN 1-55583-495-7

FOR
RICK DAVIS,
WHO HAS INSPIRED MANY QUESTIONS,
AND
RICHARD AMMON, PH.D.,
WHO HAS INSPIRED MANY ANSWERS

"I keep six honest serving men
(They taught me all I knew);
Their names are What and Why and When
And How and Where and Who."

—Rudyard Kipling

acknowledgments

From the moment I first began talking about writing a book of questions geared exclusively toward gay men, the level of interest and encouragement among the people in my life—both gay and straight—was inspiring.

I first want to thank Veston Rowe and Jack Herzberg. Veston's voice and vision resonate throughout this book, and I can't thank him enough for his enthusiasm and generosity of spirit. Jack's wit and wisdom have been an indelible influence in my life over the past nine years, and his contribution to the tone and content of this book has been significant.

I'm grateful as well to a stalwart circle of other close friends—Kiko Rodriguez, Ali Fadakar, Michael Foxworthy, Gary Costa, Janet Eastman, and Joyce Pederson—whose willingness to read, listen to, and critique various versions of this material went far beyond the call of friendship. Their presence in my life is truly a gift.

I appreciate and thank my friend Steven Fisher for his encouragement and for introducing me to my agents, Alan Nevins and Steven Rowley. Their belief in this book was energizing, and their tenacity in finding it a good home was impressive.

I also want to express my appreciation to Alyson publisher Greg Constante for giving this project the green light and to editor Gerry Kroll, whose unwavering determination to keep the material focused and "gay-specific" resulted in a better book. I value his judgment, his collaborative spirit, and his positive influence on the finished product.

Thank you to Oscar Alfaro, William Brown, David Crain, Daniel Franco, Marc LaFont, Ron Kipke, Jimmy Montoya, Peter Ochoa, and Jay Pettus for prompting me over the past ten years to explore tough questions and to Richard Ammon, Ph.D.; Andrew Berner, Ph.D.; the late Rob Eichberg, Ph.D.; Herman M. Frankel, MD; the Rev. Tari Lennon, Ph.D.; Ellen McGrath, Ph.D.; Ron Russell, Ph.D.; Reyn Sheffer; and Jean Staeheli for urging me to look beyond the easy answers.

My family has always been there for me. My thanks and love to Ruth Lawrence, Jan Knudten, Daniel Holderman,

Dorothy Sebell, Leonard Sebell, Jim Holderman, Kathy Holderman, Rachele Cost, Judy Eratostene, Nellie Jackson, and Clara Spalding. Special thanks to my grandmothers, Zelma Dolph and Alice Holderman, who I suspect would have gotten a kick out of this book once their hearts stopped racing, and to my grandfathers, Harold Dolph and Gerald Holderman, who I can say with certainty wouldn't have gotten much of a kick out of it at all.

Many others have encouraged and inspired me over the years through their words and actions. My thanks to Steve Bailey; Jim Bates; Patricia Bell; Brady Benton; Michael Bertsch; Kate Navin Booth; Fred Borenstein; Terry Branoff; Rob Bregoff; Victor Caponpon; Martin Carlson; Xavier Cervantes; Ernest Cisneros; Dave Cole; Dave Cotelessa; Steve Cox; Doris Davis; Belinda DeLong; Xavier Espinoza; Viki Eubank; Pam Felix; John Foster, MD; Sonya Friedman, Ph.D.; Alex Garcia; Lowell Gibbs; Michael Gibson; Eileen Gomez; Moana Grochow; Frank Groff; Terry Grossman; Dee Dee Hanson; Jack Hanson; Laurie Hodges; Megan Hodges; Dave Hoen; Lance Huante; John Humphrey; Maxine Humphrey; Barry Johnson;

Carolyn Johnson; Cynthia Juno; Jill Kasofsky; Jeff Kaufman; Michael Kezsely; Alan Kosher; Scott Lawrence; Neil Linsk; Jay Marzullo; Janie O'Brien Moore; Sandeep Mukherjee; Priscilla Munro; William Nagel; Mary Beth Nelson; Rob Neuneker; Phil Ochoa; Deborah Olson; Jared Olson-Gomez; Tony Ortale; Gary Parks; Gary Parsons; Trena Parsons; Jon Purdue; Jennifer Rogers; Kirwan Rockefeller, Ph.D.; Rafael Rosario, Manny Rosas; Ken Sakata; Amy Sear; Sandy Silver; Scott McBride Smith, Ph.D.; Tyrone Smith; Gwen Stewart; Bob Stohr; Duncan Strauss; Cheryl Thompson; Jerry Thompson; Patty Thompson; Joyce Ukropina; Javier Villalobos; Honey Ward; Henry Wexler, Ph.D.; and Kathy Willits.

Last but certainly never least, I want to express my gratitude and my love to Rick Davis and to Charlotte, who were both there every step of the way.

introduction

A friend once speculated that my first word was "Why?" I don't doubt it. By the time I was five years old, my curiosity was insatiable, my need to know was voracious, and "Because I said so" had been forever banished as an acceptable answer. Whether I was grilling my grandmother about why our neighbor wore high heels while picking her plum tree or insisting that my mother explain why Curly and Larry never ducked whenever Moe started to swing, inquiring minds like mine wanted to know.

It wasn't until kindergarten that I discovered not everyone found my natural curiosity attractive. One day while walking home from school with my grandfather, I interrogated him about his day at work. He eventually became exasperated with my rapid-fire questions, looked me square in the eye, and barked, "You sure are a *nosy* little bastard!"

Even back then I much preferred the word *inquisitive*. But while my grandfather didn't necessarily consider curiosity a virtue, one of my favorite teachers did. Agnes Griffith was a woman who insisted there was no such thing as a stupid question. And while I've proved her wrong more than once, I'm convinced that a well-asked question is not only the most efficient, direct way of acquiring information but also the best way to stimulate conversations that help us better understand other people and ourselves.

This book, in fact, is the result of questions first asked nearly two years ago during a memorable dinner in Laguna Beach, California, with four close friends. The idea for *Gay Questions* had been percolating for some time. That evening I posed several sample questions. By the end of a provocative, revealing dinner conversation that was peppered with "What if"s and "Have you ever"s, we had clearly gotten to know one another better than ever. By the time we'd finished dessert, I was convinced that a book featuring the kinds of questions we'd spent the evening answering could — and would — appeal to an audience far beyond that table.

Everyone I talked with, however, was certain that such a book had "already been done." It hadn't. Sure, there are plenty of books that *answer* questions for gay men, including one that offers "rules" on everything from courtship to coming out to planning a commitment ceremony. Another shares "instructions" on how to live a "fulfilling gay life." There's even a book that provides advice on "how to be affectionate" and how to negotiate household chores.

What didn't exist, until now, is a book that challenges you and other gay men to clarify your values, evaluate your judgments, examine your beliefs, and explore why you see the world the way you do. That's exactly what *Gay Questions* is designed to help you do. As you make your way through this book, you'll encounter 218 thought-provoking, stimulating, sometimes outrageous questions, the answers to which will provide a revealing glimpse into the way you think and feel about issues vital to the lives of gay men today.

Read *Gay Questions* alone and enjoy an intensely personal journey of self-discovery. Answer the questions among a group of friends and watch the sparks fly. The conversations that result are sure to be as lively as they are revealing. You'll quickly discover how dramatically your opinions and attitudes differ from those closest to you — as well as how much you all have in common. Either way, don't be surprised if you find yourself thinking and communicating more openly and honestly than ever before.

So what are you waiting for? If you think the questions are intriguing, just wait until you hear the answers.

Jerry Holderman
Los Angeles

GAY QUESTIONS

You're walking along a secluded beach early one morning when you spot a famous actor sitting on the sand with his arm around another man. Although you've always assumed the actor was gay, he's never disclosed his sexual orientation and appears at Hollywood premieres and awards shows in the company of women. He and his companion don't notice you — they've started to kiss. You happen to have a camera. Do you take his photograph or respect his privacy and keep walking? If you do snap the shot, what would you do with it? Would your decision be different if the actor recently made headlines after a bitchy antigay diatribe on a late-night TV talk show?

GAY QUESTIONS

2

You and a friend are at a movie. When one of the characters in the film is gay-bashed, two high school jocks sitting directly in front of you erupt in whistles and applause. What, if anything, would you do or say? As offended as you might be by their behavior, do they have a right to find the scene entertaining?

3

How many men would you estimate you've had sex with in your lifetime? Do you think the tally on your "encounter counter" is higher or lower than that of other men your age?

GAY QUESTIONS

4

Would you rather have a six-month love affair that was exciting, intense, and passionate or a six-year relationship that was stable, comfortable, and predictable?

5

If you could trade places for one week with any gay man living today, who would it be? What intrigues you most about his life? In what ways do you think it differs most significantly from yours? What do you think you would learn about life — and yourself — during those seven days in someone else's skin?

GAY QUESTIONS

You're at your local video store and wander into the "adult" section. You're surprised when you see a nude picture of a man on a video box who bears a remarkable resemblance to a friend of yours. You decide to rent the video and are stunned when you recognize a familiar tattoo on the actor's right arm. Your friend is quite conservative these days, and in the three years you've known each other, he's never mentioned his cinematic exploits. Do you tell him you saw his video, or do you respect his apparent desire to leave the past in the past? In either case, would you mention your discovery to mutual friends?

GAY QUESTIONS

7

You're staying at a gay hotel in Palm Springs. It's noon, and six guys are chatting in the hot tub. You can see that none of them are wearing swimsuits. Would you feel comfortable dropping your suit and climbing in? Would you find it more or less intimidating if the men happened to be casual acquaintances or friends of yours? Would you be more or less inclined to get naked at midnight?

GAY QUESTIONS

Someone you care about very much is dying. He explains that if his quality of life diminishes to a point where he no longer chooses to live, he intends to take an overdose of prescription medication. He has a supply stashed in his apartment and tells you where it is. He also asks you to promise that if he's physically unable to administer the fatal dose, you will hand it to him. Is this a promise you would be willing to make? Is it a promise you think you could keep?

GAY QUESTIONS

You're meeting your boyfriend of six months at his place. He pages you to say he's running a half hour late. You let yourself in with a key he's given you and use the time to make flight reservations for an upcoming trip. As you're sitting at his desk, you notice his phone bill lists nearly $100 in recent calls to a phone-sex line. Do you mention your discovery when he arrives?

GAY QUESTIONS

10

You and five friends are on vacation together. You pick up a gay magazine and notice that a sex survey has been completed by one of your friends. By reading the answers, do you think you could determine which of your friends had taken the survey?

11

If sexual performance were an event at the Gay Games, in which event would you be most likely to capture a gold medal? In which event might you fail to qualify for the finals?

GAY QUESTIONS

12

Do you ever fantasize about other men while making love to your partner or boyfriend? Would it bother you to discover he was having fantasies while making love with you? If you could "listen in" to discover what those fantasies were, would you do it? Do you think doing so would more likely help or hurt your relationship?

GAY QUESTIONS

13

Q: *What does a lesbian bring on the second date?*
A: A U-Haul.
Q: *What does a gay man bring on a second date?*
A: What second date?

It's an old joke but one many gay men and lesbians believe rings true. Would you agree that gay men are generally slower to commit than lesbians? If so, why do you think this is true?

GAY QUESTIONS

14

You're shopping with your boyfriend and his precocious six-year-old nephew. You and the nephew head toward the toy department while your boyfriend tries on suits. Halfway up the escalator, the little guy suddenly asks, "So do you sleep in the same bed as Uncle Jim?" How do you respond?

GAY QUESTIONS

15

"Some people say 'I love you' as though they were asking you to pass the salt," observes Steven Petrow, author of *The Essential Book of Gay Manners and Etiquette*. To how many men have you uttered these three words? In retrospect, do you still think it was love?

16

Would you be willing to abstain from sex for three years if, at the end of that time, it meant the discovery of an AIDS vaccine?

GAY QUESTIONS

17

You're having dinner with Steve and Jordan when Steve mentions that a mutual friend was arrested Saturday night. It seems that Ed and a trick decided to take a walk on the wild side in a local park. They were arrested for lewd conduct and held in jail overnight until friends bailed them out. Steve considers the arrest an injustice and cites it as "one more example of how gays are persecuted." Jordan disagrees. "I feel bad for Ed, but if you're going to jerk off in public," he argues, "you take your chances — no matter how late or how dark it is." Steve and Jordan turn to you and ask, "What do you think?" Well?

GAY QUESTIONS

18

Have you ever had sex with someone because it was easier than saying no?

19

Are there any gay public figures whose style, behavior, or approach you believe does the cause of gay rights more harm than good?

GAY QUESTIONS

20

You've met a guy through a computer bulletin board chat room and are looking forward to meeting him for coffee. When he introduces himself, you're stunned. The man who insisted that he resembles Robert Downey Jr. turns out to be a dead ringer for *Morton* Downey Jr. Though you've enjoyed chatting with him on the board, you're annoyed that he so blatantly misrepresented himself. Would you leave or stay? In either event, would you tell him how you feel?

GAY QUESTIONS

21

Gary is one of the most fun-loving practical jokers you know. The two of you are walking to his apartment when you notice more than a dozen parked cars bearing PAT BUCHANAN FOR PRESIDENT IN 2000 bumper stickers. Gary explains that one of his neighbors is "an incurable fundamentalist" who regularly hosts political fund-raisers. Gary starts chuckling, and you can tell he's up to no good even before he announces his idea. He wants to rush to a nearby gay bookstore and buy a stack of HATE IS NOT A FAMILY VALUE bumper stickers. He proposes a "sneak attack" in which the two of you would apply them to the bumpers, covering the Buchanan stickers. Would you do it? If not, why?

GAY QUESTIONS

22

You overhear a conversation at the gym in which one man tells another that Joe, a friend you see every few weeks, recently tested HIV-positive. "Don't breathe a word of it," he says. "I don't think he wants anyone to know." Would you call Joe? Would you mention the conversation you overheard or simply create an opportunity for him to talk with you if he chooses? Would you say anything to the indiscreet gossip?

GAY QUESTIONS

23

You've been listening to a new talk show on your favorite radio station and don't like what you hear. The host repeatedly refers to openly gay men as "admitted homosexuals" and calls children and hemophiliacs "the innocent AIDS victims." Would you call the show and challenge the host on-air? Write a letter to station management? Send protest letters to the program's sponsors? Alert the Gay and Lesbian Alliance Against Defamation? Tune in another station? Continue listening in order to document the host's offensive comments? Do nothing?

GAY QUESTIONS

24

If you suddenly became famous and one of your friends were to write a "tell-all" exposé, which friend would have the most ammunition?

25

Have you ever paid for sex? (Dinner doesn't count!)

GAY QUESTIONS

26

After a dating dry spell, you decide to give the gay classifieds a try. You've scanned the ads and circled those that most interest you. When you ask a friend to look them over, his observation startles you: He notes that you've circled ads placed only by men of your same race and/or nationality. He suggests that you're ethnocentric at best and racist at worst. Does he have a point?

GAY QUESTIONS

27

How do you define the difference between a trick, an affair, and a date?

28

If scientists developed a pill that would safely and permanently change your sexual orientation from gay to straight, would you consider taking it? If not, was there *ever* a time when you would have gladly swallowed the pill? When? Why?

GAY QUESTIONS

29

Claudia and Jayne are your favorite lesbians. They're equally fond of you and have approached you with a proposal. After nine years together, they've decided to have a baby. While a sperm bank is one option, they'd prefer a more direct deposit — yours. They explain that if you agree to be the sperm donor, there would be no strings attached. You would sign away all parental rights and responsibilities. They ask you to consider their proposal and invite you to brunch the following weekend. What considerations would factor into your decision? What would that decision be? Are there other circumstances in which you would consider donating sperm?

GAY QUESTIONS

30

What's the tackiest pickup line anyone's ever used on you? How about the sexiest? The most effective? What are the tackiest, sexiest, and most effective lines *you've* ever used?

31

Does the idea of living in a predominantly gay area — such as Greenwich Village, West Hollywood, Key West, or the Castro district — appeal to you? Do you think you would tire of it? What do you think would be the benefits and drawbacks of life in a "gay ghetto"?

GAY QUESTIONS

32

You've befriended a gay man who just turned eighteen. He trusts you and loves regaling you with details about his latest sexual conquests. You become concerned about his health and safety when he divulges that he's engaging in unsafe sex and sex in high-risk public places. Each time you voice your concerns, he promises to be more careful. But every time the two of you talk, it's clear his behavior hasn't changed. You happen to know his uncle, who is also gay. Would you betray the young man's confidence by discussing your concerns with his uncle in hopes that he can communicate with his nephew in a way you've been unable to?

GAY QUESTIONS

33

You're a sucker for the preppy, conservative look. For the past month you have dated a man who's right up your alley — or so you thought. Tonight's the big night, and as you unbutton his crisply starched Polo shirt, you're shocked by what you discover — a pair of nipple rings and a huge skull and crossbones tattooed on his chest. The coup de grâce awaits beneath his khakis: a thick silver ring pierces the head of his penis. What do you say? What do you do?

GAY QUESTIONS

34

What do you think is your family's greatest misconception about being gay? Have you ever discussed it with them? If you're out to your parents, how have their attitudes toward homosexuality changed since you told them?

GAY QUESTIONS

35

You're strolling through the courtyard of a gay hotel late one night when you pass by a window and notice two men engaged in very intense, passionate sex. They've pulled the vertical blinds at an angle but apparently don't realize that the mirrored closet doors afford anyone who walks by an unobstructed view of the hot action. Do you stop and watch — or do you keep walking? Would your decision be different if the blinds were left open and the guys clearly relished the idea of being watched? Would you watch if it were a straight couple? Two lesbians?

GAY QUESTIONS

36

An openly gay candidate is locked in a fierce battle to unseat your congressman, who happens to have a solid record on gay rights and other issues that matter to you. Do you shift your support to the gay candidate simply because he's gay?

37

You're on vacation, and a wealthy, average-looking older man tells you you're his fantasy come true. He offers you $10,000 in cash to spend one night with him. No one would find out unless you mentioned it. Would you consider it? Why or why not?

GAY QUESTIONS

38

Alice Longworth once said, "If you can't say anything good about someone, sit right here by me." Would you say you enjoy gossip more than, as much as, or less than most people you know? Would you rather share gossip or hear it? When, if ever, do you think gossip is wrong?

39

If you were treated to a grooming and wardrobe makeover by a top stylist, what changes do you think he'd be most likely to recommend?

GAY QUESTIONS

"For Christ's sake, open your mouths," Bette Midler once urged her gay fans. "Don't you people ever get tired of being stepped on?" When is the last time you stood up — or spoke up — for your rights as a gay man?

GAY QUESTIONS

41

Sam, a neighbor who tested HIV-positive a year ago, asks your opinion on a subject that's got him stumped. When, he wonders, do you think it's appropriate to reveal his HIV status to someone he's dating? "If I tell him before he gets to know me," he explains, "it becomes an easy excuse for him to split. Yet if I wait too long, he might feel betrayed." What advice do you give?

GAY QUESTIONS

42

According to an informal national survey cited by Kevin DiLallo and Jack Krumholtz, the authors of *The Unofficial Gay Manual*, the top ten turnoffs of men searching for Prince Charming are: femmes, attitude, self-absorption, bad bodies, unsightly body hair, smoking, cologne overdose, no sense of humor, poor taste in clothes, and — brace yourself — drinking with a straw. Which three top your list of turnoffs? What would you add to the list?

GAY QUESTIONS

43

Do you think it's possible for two men to stay in a long-term sexually monogamous relationship? Is it desirable? Why or why not?

44

Given a choice of having sex with a beautiful woman or a gay man you found totally unappealing, which would you choose?

GAY QUESTIONS

45

The maître d' at one of your favorite restaurants is "Mr. February" in a popular nude gay calendar. You've seen it and now fully appreciate why the tuxedoed stud walks proud. Even though you've been joking with friends during dinner about the revealing photograph, you can't believe it when one of them waves the calendar boy over to your table and says, "I just saw your calendar — and honey, no matter what *anyone* says, February is *not* the shortest month of the year!" Would you be embarrassed or amused?

GAY QUESTIONS

46

You're falling in love with a man who has expressed interest in adopting children. Would you consider this an obstacle or an opportunity?

47

On a first date, do you prefer to pick up the check, let the other guy treat, or go dutch? Why?

GAY QUESTIONS

48

As you board a flight to Washington, D.C., you notice a notoriously homophobic U.S. senator occupying the seat next to yours. Would you ask the flight attendant to move you, sit in your assigned seat and ignore him, or use this curious twist of fate as an opportunity to lobby one of the gay movement's most vitriolic, powerful opponents?

GAY QUESTIONS

49

You're strolling through a local gay pride festival when you spot a business client in the crowd. Until now it never occurred to you that he might be gay. You're fairly sure — but not certain — that he saw you, but he's turned away and is walking in the opposite direction. Do you attempt to catch up with him, or do trust your hunch that he didn't want to be seen? If you don't talk with him at the festival, do you say anything the next time you visit his office?

GAY QUESTIONS

50

How important is it to you that your friends approve of a man you're dating? If several of them made it clear that they didn't care for him, would you reconsider seeing him again?

51

When a man tells you he's HIV-negative, do you take him at his word or assume that everyone is positive and take what you consider appropriate precautions?

GAY QUESTIONS

52

Would you rather spend an evening at the Mr. International Leather Contest or the Diva Drag Queen Pageant?

53

A buddy from the gym invites you to a party he's throwing Saturday night. The theme? "Truth or Dare." Though he insists otherwise, you're fairly certain it's going to turn into a group sex scene. Do you go? What do you do if it turns out you were right?

GAY QUESTIONS

54

You're at a party, and one of the other guests makes a flagrant pass at your lover. Are you more likely to be amused, flattered, or angry?

55

You and Mr. Right decide to live together. On the lease application you're asked the relationship between you and the coapplicant. What do you write down? Partner? Boyfriend? Lover? Husband? Significant other? Spouse? Roommate? Friend? Companion? Mate?

GAY QUESTIONS

56

What sexual fantasies haven't you fulfilled? Why not?

57

How much older than you was the oldest man you've ever dated? How much younger was the youngest? Which of these experiences do you remember most fondly?

GAY QUESTIONS

58

Does your doctor know you're gay? Why have you — or haven't you — chosen to tell him or her?

59

At this point in your life, what do you treasure most — good friends, good food, good sex, or good theater tickets? Would you have answered this question differently a year ago? Five years ago?

GAY QUESTIONS

What's more important to you in a relationship — sexual monogamy or emotional fidelity? Why?

An acquaintance repeatedly refers to your best female friend as a "fag hag." Are you offended? Do you say anything?

GAY QUESTIONS

62

As you're chatting on the Internet with a guy who calls himself "YoungLuvn," it becomes clear that he has misread your age — 31 — as 13 and thinks he's communicating with a teenage boy. The conversation turns sexual, and he suggests you meet him after school at a local video arcade and then go to his place. Would you report him to the system operator and/or the police? If you did and were asked to cooperate in a police sting to help catch the pedophile, would you do it?

GAY QUESTIONS

63

Have you ever been tormented, threatened, intimidated, or stalked by a former date, boyfriend, or lover after your relationship ended? How did you deal with the situation?

64

Four of your closest friends are playing cards one night while you're out of town. You somehow become the topic of conversation. What three words are most often used to describe your personality?

GAY QUESTIONS

65

During one of the breaks in a daytime talk show, a promo runs for an upcoming episode: "We Haven't Seen Each Other in Years — And I Have Something to Tell You." You call the 800 number and explain that you had a wild crush on your best friend from high school but never told him. The two of you lost touch and haven't talked in years. When one of the show's producers calls back, she says she loves your story. She explains she'll contact your high school buddy and invite him to New York to be a guest but that the subject of the show won't be revealed to him until the two of you meet face-to-face onstage. It's an all-expenses paid trip to New York — and an opportunity to reunite with your buddy, but you're concerned your friend might not welcome your news. What do you do?

GAY QUESTIONS

66

At what age do you first remember being attracted to other boys or men? Was there a particular person who sparked this initial attraction, or was it more of a general feeling?

67

Which song or movie title best describes your love life?

GAY QUESTIONS

When you were a kid, were you teased about any physical characteristics? Did you have any nicknames? If so, how do you think those early experiences shaped how you feel about and see yourself today?

Which do you find more uncomfortable — being rejected or telling another man you're not interested in seeing him again?

GAY QUESTIONS

70

You're using the rest room at a local mall. As you begin to zip up, a man enters and stands at the urinal next to you. You're washing your hands when he announces, "Police. You're under arrest." He writes a bogus report in which he alleges a sexual contact that did not occur. Realizing that it will boil down to your word against the officer's, do you fight on principle and go to court, or do you plea bargain, pay the fine, and chalk it up to a one-two punch of bad luck and bad timing?

GAY QUESTIONS

71

It's your first anniversary, and you've told your boyfriend you're planning something special. You're determined to create a romantic evening he'll never forget. What do you do?

72

What three physical characteristics do you first notice when meeting another man?

GAY QUESTIONS

73

Would you consider dating a man whose political perspective was the polar opposite of yours? How important is it to you that a potential partner share a similar political view of the world?

74

Do you believe you were born gay? Is sexual orientation a choice or a fact? Does it matter to you?

GAY QUESTIONS

75

You and your lover have agreed to a monogamous relationship. If he broke the agreement and had a one-night stand while away on a business trip, would you want to know about it? Why or why not?

76

How has your taste in men changed since you first came out? Would you have dated your partner or most recent boyfriend back then? Do you think you'd still be interested in your first boyfriend if you met him for the first time today?

GAY QUESTIONS

77

Do you think successful, high-profile gay men and lesbians have a moral obligation to come out, or is it a personal decision each person must make for himself or herself?

78

What do you know about relationships today that you wish you'd known five years ago?

GAY QUESTIONS

79

Many gay men who aren't in a relationship say they wish they were. Based on your experience, why do you think most men who say they want a relationship aren't in one?

80

Would you consider going on a blind date arranged by a straight couple who knew you well?

GAY QUESTIONS

81

"Are you gay?" Has anyone ever asked you this question point-blank? How did you respond? Did you find their directness refreshing or intrusive? Have you ever bluntly asked this question yourself?

82

On a scale of one to ten (ten being best), how attractive do you consider yourself? How intelligent? How sexually talented? How socially aware?

GAY QUESTIONS

83

Have you ever called a phone-sex line? If so, did you exaggerate or embellish your description of yourself when talking with other men?

84

Who usually says "I love you" first — him or you?

GAY QUESTIONS

85

Have you ever loved two men at the same time?

86

The new teller at your bank gets your blood racing faster than an unattended stack of $100 bills. You're not sure whether he's cruising you or it's just wishful thinking. How would you go about finding out whether his interest rate rivals yours?

GAY QUESTIONS

87

Have you ever dated a man whose HIV status you knew was different from yours? If so, what issues did it raise for both of you?

88

Is there ever a time when outing — publicly disclosing a person's sexual orientation against his or her will — is appropriate?

GAY QUESTIONS

There are those who believe the best way to neutralize homophobic epithets like "faggot" or "queer" is to reclaim them and adopt them in gay jargon as terms of endearment. What do you think of this strategy? Do you find such words emotionally charged? Are you offended by them? Does your reaction depend on who's using them and/or the context?

GAY QUESTIONS

Do you ever discuss intimate details about your sex life with friends? Would it bother you to discover your boyfriend does?

What's your favorite gay-themed film or play? What message does it convey?

GAY QUESTIONS

92

Do you think it's possible to be emotionally monogamous in a sexually open relationship?

93

If you died unexpectedly today, how long would you want your lover to wait before he began dating again? If your lover died unexpectedly, how long would you wait before dating again? How long do you think he'd want you to wait?

GAY QUESTIONS

94

It's early November, and your mother calls. The conversation turns to Thanksgiving. You tell her you'd like to invite the man you've been dating since January, but she says, "I don't think that would be a good idea." Do you respect her wishes and go alone or decline the invitation and prepare turkey dinner at home for you and your boyfriend? In either event, do you discuss your concerns with your mother? Your boyfriend?

GAY QUESTIONS

95

If you could snap your fingers and magically either lose twenty pounds, drop ten years from your age, or add three inches to the length of your penis, which would you choose?

96

What one personality trait do the men you've dated tend to possess?

GAY QUESTIONS

97

How many gay T-shirts (you know, I'M NOT GAY, BUT MY BOYFRIEND IS) do you own? Do you wear them only to gay events or as everyday attire? Have you ever felt uncomfortable or conspicuous while wearing one?

98

Do you think society is generally more accepting of lesbians or gay men? Why?

GAY QUESTIONS

99

An acquaintance makes headlines after reporting a gay bashing in which his apartment was vandalized. You've known the man for years and recall an identical incident that allegedly happened to him eight years ago in another city where you both lived. You suspect he has staged the attack in order to boost his name recognition in an upcoming local city council election. What, if anything, would you say or do?

GAY QUESTIONS

100

You introduce two men at a barbecue. At an event several months later, you learn they've been dating ever since. During the evening both reveal their feelings in separate conversations. One has fallen head over heels in love and is certain the feelings are mutual. The other clearly sees it as a casual friendship with consensual sex and nothing more. Do you intervene or let nature take its course? If you were to say something, to whom would you say it?

GAY QUESTIONS

101

If you could travel to another time and place to experience firsthand what gay life was like then, what era and which locale would you choose to visit?

102

Do you think same-sex marriage will be legalized nationally during your lifetime? Do you believe it should be? Why or why not?

GAY QUESTIONS

103

Would you choose to legally marry if you had the opportunity?

104

"If gay marriages were legal when I was coming out," jokes your pal Morgan, "I'd have more ex-husbands than Elizabeth Taylor!" If same-sex marriage had always been legal, do you think you would be married right now? To how many former boyfriends would you have been willing to say "I do"?

GAY QUESTIONS

105

You and a group of friends are on a camping trip. The campfire conversation has run the gamut from provocative political discussion to truly tasteless jokes when one of the guys suggests you play a revealing game he calls "Ultimate Orgy." He names five famous men he would invite to his ultimate orgy. Now it's your turn. Who would top (or bottom) your guest list?

GAY QUESTIONS

106

Do you think most of the men you've dated have been more or less intelligent than you? More or less physically attractive? More or less outgoing?

107

What's the longest you've ever gone without sex? Was it by choice? What were the circumstances?

GAY QUESTIONS

108

Have you ever felt sexually compulsive? What behavior caused you concern? How would you define the difference between sexual activity and sexual addiction?

109

Several weeks after becoming fast friends with a man you met at a seminar, he reveals he has lymphoma and a life expectancy of less than six months. Would his revelation influence your interest in developing the friendship? Would you be more likely to withdraw or proceed?

GAY QUESTIONS

110

Your lover of three years revealed his boot fetish to you six months ago. While you don't share his predilection, you've agreed to his occasional request that you "boot up" during sex. Lately, however, your desire to play "Ride 'Em Cowboy" has diminished, while his has increased. Your lover thinks you're uptight. You think his fetish has become an obsession. Are you more likely to "grin and wear it," tell him that enough is enough, or try to find some middle ground?

GAY QUESTIONS

111

Are you pee-shy? If so, why?

112

If a series of sexual-technique seminars were offered at your local gay and lesbian community center, which session would you want your lover not to miss? Which one would he want you to enroll in?

GAY QUESTIONS

113

You and a friend are strolling down Bourbon Street during Mardi Gras. A group of guys on a balcony urge you to drop your pants in exchange for beads. Do you do it?

114

Have you ever been involved with a man who earned significantly more or less money than you? Did the disparity in income create significant challenges or obstacles? If so, how did you resolve them?

GAY QUESTIONS

115

"Sex is like bridge," female impersonator Charles Pierce once noted. "If you don't have a good partner, you'd better have a good hand." During the past seven days, how many times have you masturbated to the point of ejaculation?

116

A friend bets you $500 that you can't stay out of gay clubs and bars for one year. Would you take him up on his bet? If so, would winning the bet prove challenging?

GAY QUESTIONS

117

You're out of town on business and strike up a conversation with a man at a subway stop. He invites you back to his place for a drink. Would you go? Would you automatically assume he was interested in sex?

GAY QUESTIONS

118

You're arranging your late friend Bill's memorial service. He wanted those attending to have a chance to share their memories and say good-bye. You're concerned that Josh, a free spirit with whom Bill shared plenty of wild times, might be indiscreet and share stories at the service that would likely make Bill's family uncomfortable. You don't want to second-guess or censor Josh's comments, yet you're concerned about the family's feelings. Would you express your concerns to Josh before the service?

GAY QUESTIONS

119

You've decided to volunteer at your local gay and lesbian community center. During your orientation you're asked to consider enrolling in a training class to become a counselor for the center's anonymous HIV testing program. You're told that delivering HIV test results is not a job for everyone. Is it a job for you? Would you be good at it? Why or why not?

GAY QUESTIONS

120

A friend calls to tell you he's recently started dating one of your former boyfriends. Would you be upset? If so, why? Would your reaction depend on which friend and which former boyfriend were involved?

121

Who is your favorite gay or lesbian author?

GAY QUESTIONS

122

Have you ever talked with an older gay man about what it was like coming out and living a gay life in another era? If so, what did you learn from that conversation?

123

What's more important to you in a partner: someone who's well-connected, well-organized, well-educated, well-groomed, well-mannered, or well-hung?

GAY QUESTIONS

124

What gift given to you by another man do you most cherish?

125

How good is your gaydar? If you were at a business reception and were told that ten of the 100 men present were gay, how many do you think your gaydar could detect by the end of the evening?

GAY QUESTIONS

126

You come home one night and find your boyfriend engaged in a sexual conversation on the Internet. Would you consider this a breach of trust in your relationship or dismiss it as harmless fun? Would your answer be different if you learned that "HungStud," the guy on the other end of the nasty exchange, lives nearby and has invited your beau to come over for some live action?

GAY QUESTIONS

127

How old were you when you had your first sexual experience? Was it with a male or a female?

128

What personality trait do you find most attractive in other gay men? Least attractive?

GAY QUESTIONS

129

Your parents are coming for a weekend visit. Do you make any effort to "straighten up" the house? If so, what items would you move or hide? Why? If not, was there once a time when such a visit would have sent you scrambling?

130

Who is your all-time favorite gay television, film, or theatrical character? What attracts you to him or her?

GAY QUESTIONS

131

Your office holiday party is coming up, and "you and a guest" are invited to the festivities. Do you invite your boyfriend or a male date, take a female friend, or go solo?

132

Are you ashamed of or embarrassed by any of your sexual fantasies?

GAY QUESTIONS

133

Six of your best friends have decided to attend this year's local Halloween celebration as finalists from the Miss Universe Pageant — and insist you would be the ultimate Miss Norway! You've never done drag and swore you never would. You planned to go as a cowboy, but they won't take no for an answer. Do you finally give in and go for it — or do you stick to your guns?

GAY QUESTIONS

134

It's been said that only when we don't need to be in a relationship are we truly ready to have one. If you're currently not in a relationship, how comfortable are you not being half of a couple? If you are in a relationship and found yourself suddenly single, would you be inclined to begin dating right away or take some time to adjust?

GAY QUESTIONS

135

A friend jokes that you're "not really gay" unless your CD collection includes music by Judy Garland, Barbra Streisand, Madonna — and at least one Broadway cast album. Based on his definition, are you a member of the club? Why do you think so many gay men are such loyal fans of singers like Garland and Streisand?

GAY QUESTIONS

136

Your company has just offered you a major promotion. It's a great career move but requires a two-year relocation to a small Midwestern city with no signs of gay life. Would you accept the offer?

137

If you could add one year to the life of a dying friend by shaving one year off your own, would you do it?

GAY QUESTIONS

138

How many of your closest friends are straight? How many are lesbians? Gay?

139

In *Torch Song Trilogy* Harvey Fierstein insists, "Gay liberation should not be a license to be a perpetual adolescent." Do you think the stereotype that many gay men refuse to grow up is an accurate one?

GAY QUESTIONS

140

The man you're dating has photographs of two former lovers displayed on a shelf in his bedroom. One of them has remained a close friend; the other died in an accident six years ago. Would the photos bother you? If so, would you discuss it?

141

How do you define "safe sex"? Which sexual activities do you consider totally safe, possibly safe, and unsafe?

GAY QUESTIONS

142

You know a couple who seem to have a loving, successful relationship, but they have a habit many of their friends find unusual. Whenever one of them is away on business — which averages one week every month or two — they choose not to speak by phone. They say they enjoy the "healthy break" from each other and that absence indeed "makes the heart grow fonder." It certainly seems to work for them. Would it work for you?

GAY QUESTIONS

143

You're having dinner with a couple of friends when the conversation becomes heated. Wayne argues that "militant fringe groups" like ACT UP "give gays a bad name," "do more harm than good," and are "totally counterproductive." Shawn couldn't disagree more. He credits such groups with using "action instead of words," "pushing the edge," and "attracting attention to issues that are vital to our community." The only thing Wayne and Shawn seem to agree on is their desire to know where *you* stand on the subject. What do you tell them?

GAY QUESTIONS

144

What sexual activity wouldn't you engage in under any circumstances? Why?

145

Have you ever declined an invitation in order to avoid an ex-lover or ex-boyfriend you knew would be attending the same event?

GAY QUESTIONS

146

You're attending a gay fund-raiser. One of the silent-auction items is a weekend at a gay resort with a porn star who happens to be your favorite. Would you bid? How much would you be willing to pay? Would you assume that sex was an implied part of the package? If a wealthy friend bid on the package and gave it to you as a gift, would you go?

147

Would you rather date a gorgeous guy who was a dud in the bedroom or an average-looking guy who was sensational between the sheets?

GAY QUESTIONS

148

Have you ever allowed anyone to take nude photographs of you or videotape you during sex? If so, were there any conditions? Did you enjoy viewing them later? Have you ever shown them to anyone? Who has possession of them now?

149

Who is the happiest gay couple you know? What do you think makes their relationship work?

GAY QUESTIONS

150

It's been said that the secret to finding a good man is to be one. All things considered, do you consider yourself a good man?

151

You've been seeing a man for two weeks when he reveals he's married and has no plans to leave his wife. He makes it clear he'd love to continue getting together. Assuming the sex was stellar, would you consider such an arrangement or would you tell Mr. Switch-hitter that he's just struck out?

GAY QUESTIONS

152

You've been dating Roy for several months and are having a terrific time. He mentions he's going away for the weekend with a friend. Would you assume that because the two of you are dating, he wouldn't have sex while he's away — or that since you have no agreements, he's free to do whatever he chooses? In either case, would you talk with him about it?

GAY QUESTIONS

153

You're having brunch with five friends when one of them says to you, "Don't look now, but the guy who just walked in is exactly your type!" The others check him out and unanimously agree. What is your "type"?

154

You're subscribing to a gay magazine and have the option of having it sent to you in a plain wrapper. If you opt for the wrapper, why?

GAY QUESTIONS

155

In *The Unofficial Gay Manual,* the authors describe a cruising technique they call the 1-2-3 Turn. That's when you pass an attractive man on the street, count to three, then look over your shoulder. "If he's interested," the authors write, "he'll turn at precisely the same moment. It's as predictable as the swallows' return to Capistrano." Have you ever done the 1-2-3 Turn? What, if anything, came of it?

GAY QUESTIONS

156

A friend of yours has developed what you consider a serious drinking problem. Would you say anything to him? If you were told to mind your own business, would you consider organizing an intervention with family members and other friends who shared your concern?

157

Have you ever gone home with a guy only to decide at some point during the evening that you'd made a terrible mistake? How did you handle the situation?

GAY QUESTIONS

158

Is there anything you'd like to know about your boyfriend's past but are afraid to ask?

159

One of your close friends is dating someone you know is HIV-positive. As he confides intimate details about their budding relationship, you realize that Mr. Boyfriend has obviously lied to your friend about his HIV status. Do you tell your friend? Would doing so be an invasion of the other man's privacy? Why or why not?

GAY QUESTIONS

What's the worst thing a boyfriend has ever done to you?

What's the worst thing you've ever done to a boyfriend?

GAY QUESTIONS

162

What one change would you most like to make in your sex life? Why haven't you already made it?

163

"I'm not a size queen — I just like 'em big," jokes your friend William. Oscar sees it differently: "It's not the size of the wand," he insists, "it's the skill of the magician." How important is size to you?

GAY QUESTIONS

164

"What immediately attracted me to Rob is the way he treats people," reports your friend Tyler. "Whether he's talking with an important client or a busboy, he's always polite and friendly. I like that." What's the first thing you noticed about your lover, boyfriend, or most recent date?

165

Do you ever enjoy being physically restrained during sex?

GAY QUESTIONS

166

You're having sex with a guy who totally turns you on — until he starts up with the dirty talk. He sounds so much like a sound track from a bad porn movie that you can't help starting to laugh. He asks what's wrong. Do you tell him you don't really like his "You like it, don'tcha"s, or do you avoid the subject and try to refocus on more urgent issues?

167

What's your favorite way to have an orgasm?

GAY QUESTIONS

168

On a scale of one to ten (one being totally butch and ten being a raging queen), where do you think most people meeting you for the first time would rank you?

169

You see a close friend's lover kissing and groping another man at a club. Would you say anything to your friend? How about to his lover?

GAY QUESTIONS

170

One night you answer the phone and are greeted by the father of a boyhood pal. For years you had a secret crush on this man. He's in town on business and is calling to invite you to dinner. You're thrilled to discover he's every bit as attractive today as he was years ago. During dinner he talks about his wife and son, whom you haven't seen in years. As he drives you home, it's obvious he's in no rush to return to his hotel — and that he's every bit as interested in you as you've always been in him. What do you do?

GAY QUESTIONS

171

Have you ever attended a gay commitment ceremony? What did — and didn't — you like about it?

172

Which do you usually find more of a turn-on — a planned lovemaking session complete with candles and music or a wild, spur-of-the-moment sexfest?

GAY QUESTIONS

173

You're having dinner in a crowded restaurant with your best friend and his new boyfriend. They're holding hands and seem oblivious to the fact that more than a few patrons are gawking at them. Would this make you uncomfortable? If so, would you say anything to your friend? Would you say anything to the people who are staring?

GAY QUESTIONS

174

When do you and your partner celebrate your anniversary: the day the two of you met, the day you first had sex, or the day you moved in together?

175

A friend invites you to a safe-sex bondage demonstration at a local S/M club. Would you go?

GAY QUESTIONS

176

Does the idea of having sex in a public place intrigue you? When's the last time you did it? Where?

177

Have you ever been in a relationship that was emotionally, physically, or sexually abusive? How long did you stay in it? Why? What prompted you to finally get out?

GAY QUESTIONS

178

When you think of stereotypical "gay careers," which three first come to mind? Do you personally know men in each of these careers? Did stereotypes encourage or discourage you from exploring these fields as career options?

179

Have you ever attended an underwear party? If you were invited to one this weekend, would you wear boxers or briefs?

GAY QUESTIONS

180

You're at a gay dance club and notice that a guy across the room is cruising you. You're intrigued, but he's not making a move. Would you approach him or wait him out?

181

Think back to your wildest, most intense sexual experience. What made it so unforgettable? Was it with a trick or with someone you loved?

GAY QUESTIONS

182

You and your lover are attending a gay awards banquet. You spot a former boyfriend you haven't seen in years sitting across the ballroom. Would you approach him or avoid him? Would you be comfortable introducing him to your lover? If not, why?

183

Have you ever seriously considered getting a tattoo or body piercing? If so, what would you have done? If you've already done it, are you glad you did?

GAY QUESTIONS

184

If a man you dated used poppers every time the two of you made love, would his apparent dependency on the inhalant bother you? Would you say anything? How would you respond if he insisted he didn't "need" poppers but found that using them simply "enhanced the experience"?

185

What have you tried sexually that you would never do again? Why?

GAY QUESTIONS

186

What's the most unusual location in which you've ever had sex?

187

Do you know anyone who is part of an ongoing three-way relationship? What was your reaction when you first learned of it? Have your feelings changed? Do you think you could ever be part of this kind of relationship?

GAY QUESTIONS

188

Have you ever felt deep down inside that a boyfriend or partner was "too good" for you — or that you were "too good" for him? How did you resolve this conflict?

189

Have you ever felt physically threatened or intimidated by a stranger because of your sexual orientation? What did you do about it?

GAY QUESTIONS

190

You discover that an HIV-positive friend has conspired with his doctor to grossly exaggerate the severity of his illness in order to reach a viatical settlement on a life insurance policy. Would you say anything to him? To the doctor? To the insurance company?

191

You and Carl have been dating for eight months. He's out of town for the weekend and asks you to drop by to feed his cat. When you do, you notice his journal on his nightstand? Would you read it?

GAY QUESTIONS

192

When you hear about a new gay-themed play, do you assume the theatrical production will feature male nudity? Do you find the trend of gay theater featuring nudity onstage to be liberating or gratuitous? Are you more or less likely to see a gay-themed play if you know it includes nudity?

193

Name three things you wish your boyfriend or partner would do more often. Less often?

GAY QUESTIONS

194

If you're currently in a relationship, do you think it's more healthy or less healthy than most relationships you've observed? How likely is it that the two of you will be together five years from now?

195

Have you saved any cards or letters from former boyfriends? If so, how often do you read them? If your partner expressed interest in reading them, would you let him? Do you keep them hidden or locked away?

GAY QUESTIONS

196

You're checking into the hospital for minor surgery. When asked whom to notify in case of emergency, you give the admissions clerk your lover's name and indicate he is your partner. When she hands you the computerized form to sign, you notice she's listed him as "friend." Do you ask her to make the correction, make the change on the form personally, or let it go?

GAY QUESTIONS

197

Are you more often sexually attracted to younger men, older men, or men around your own age? Why?

198

You meet a man you absolutely adore. The catch? He's from Australia and is in town on a short-term work project. He's up-front in telling you that in six months he'll be returning to Sydney — the city, not a man. He's equally candid in expressing his desire to "get to know you much, much better." What do you do? Is it better to love and lose or not to love at all?

GAY QUESTIONS

199

You're having lunch with friends at a new gay restaurant. The food is uninspired, and the waiter exudes more attitude than RuPaul. One of your friends isn't surprised. He argues that most gay restaurants, hotels, and stores he's patronized have left him convinced that gay businesses generally offer less quality for more money. What's more, he insists, they tend to take their customers for granted. Do you agree or disagree? Do you ever frequent gay businesses that offer marginal service simply because they attract a gay crowd?

GAY QUESTIONS

200

You've known Dan and Judy since college and count them among your closest friends, so you're thrilled when they call to tell you they'll be in town tomorrow night. There's only one problem — you've already accepted an invitation to a birthday party. When you call the host to ask whether he'd mind if you bring Dan and Judy along, he tells you it's a "gay party" and that he'd rather keep it that way. Do you cancel your party plans or go and then meet up with the out-of-towners later? Would you be offended that your friends weren't welcome simply because they aren't gay? Would you say anything?

GAY QUESTIONS

201

Do you tend to feel more self-conscious in a group of gay men or straight men?

202

Have you ever dated a man from another ethnic group? If not, why? Do you date men only from a different ethnic group? If so, why?

GAY QUESTIONS

203

According to Fran Lebowitz, gay culture is American culture. "If you removed all the homosexuals and homosexual influence from what is generally regarded as American culture," she says, "you would pretty much be left with *Let's Make a Deal.*" In what areas do you think gay men have most contributed to American culture?

GAY QUESTIONS

204

French writer André Gide once said, "It is better to be hated for what one is than loved for what one is not." In contemplating your coming out as a gay man, whose love did or do you most fear losing? If you have already come out, whose reaction caught you most off-guard? Was it surprisingly positive or negative?

GAY QUESTIONS

205

You're waiting for friends at a gay dance club when a sassy drag queen named Eureka Fish sits down and strikes up a thoroughly entertaining conversation. You glance at your watch and realize your friends should be there any minute. Do you continue talking with Miss Eureka and introduce her when they arrive, or are you concerned enough about what your friends might say or think that you intentionally end the conversation before they show up?

GAY QUESTIONS

206

You've just returned from an out-of-town gay conference where you met several terrific men. A beautiful floral arrangement sent by a "secret admirer" awaits you. You know the florist and could find out who sent the flowers if you really wanted to know. Would you be more likely to make the call or enjoy the guessing game and the mystery of the moment?

GAY QUESTIONS

207

A friend of yours who's been living with AIDS for many years is experiencing a rapid decline in health. He confides that he's planning to attend an antigay rally spearheaded by a virulent religious homophobe — and that he's taking a gun with him. Your friend rationalizes that he has nothing to lose and argues that his assassination plot would be the ultimate political statement. Would you attempt to talk him out of it? If you were certain he intended to follow through with his plan, would you alert the authorities or let fate run its course? If you did remain silent and your friend made good on his threat, do you think you would feel any moral responsibility or remorse?

GAY QUESTIONS

208

Phil is one of your best friends, but he's always been a tad possessive in relationships. He calls you one afternoon and explains that he returned home early from work to find his lover of three years masturbating to a porn video. He's livid and insists that "when two guys are in a relationship, jerking off to a video of hot men is no different from having sex with some trick!" Are you more likely to agree or to tell Phil to get a grip?

GAY QUESTIONS

209

Would the boy you once were be proud of the man you've become?

210

Would you consider dating a closeted gay man who made it clear that he had no intention of coming out and that any relationship he entered into would need to be "discreet" and very "low profile"?

GAY QUESTIONS

211

There's only one problem with your friend Patrick: He's the goddess of "girlfriend talk." Every conversation seems to be peppered with comments like "She's such a fag" and "That big queer is such a girl!" You know Patrick has a heart of gold and that his comments aren't intended to be malicious, but you find yourself growing increasingly intolerant of his catty chatter. Do you tell him how you feel, or do you let it go and remind yourself that everyone has his own style?

GAY QUESTIONS

212

What do you consider to be the most gay-friendly city in the world? Is your opinion based on personal experience or reputation?

213

Have you ever said "I love you" to another man when you really didn't mean it? If so, why?

GAY QUESTIONS

214

You're talking with two coworkers about an upcoming AIDS fund-raiser. Victor says he's decided to pass because "the epidemic is essentially over." Martin adamantly disagrees and argues that "we're a long way from being able to talk about AIDS in the past tense." Who's right?

215

In a crowded room of gay men, are you more likely to blend in or stand out? Why?

GAY QUESTIONS

216

Is being self-revealing about your sexual orientation always necessary? It's a question you have to answer when you receive a surprise phone call from Glenda, the first girl you ever kissed. You haven't talked with her since high school, and it soon becomes clear that your lives have taken very different paths. She's visiting your city — 2,000 miles from where the two of you grew up — with her husband and seven kids to perform at a Christian Family Choir Festival. She thinks it would be "such a blessing" to see you again. You have a hunch, however, that she won't be singing "Hallelujah" when you tell her you're gay. Do you accept her invitation? If so, do you volunteer details about your life?

GAY QUESTIONS

217

Three days before he dies, your friend Paul tells you there's a letter in his desk and asks you to deliver it upon his death to Ken, his former lover. You find the letter, which is a bitter, blaming recitation of what went wrong with their relationship. Paul and Ken's breakup was high drama, but in recent years they'd become friendly again. In fact, Ken visited Paul the day before he died. You know the letter will break Ken's heart and question the point of delivering it, yet you feel an obligation to honor Paul's wishes. What do you do?

GAY QUESTIONS

218

An older openly gay actor friend of yours is nominated for an Academy Award and invites you to be his guest at the gala. He warns that photographs of the two of you will inevitably end up in the tabloids and that you'll undoubtedly be branded his new "boy toy." He couldn't care less. Would you? If so, would your concern be great enough to keep you from going?

GAY QUESTIONS

219

It's New Year's morning. You wake up naked with a horrendous hangover—and your roommate's boyfriend! You're the first one up; your roommate, his boyfriend, and several friends who have stayed over are still fast asleep. You read the morning paper and try to remember what happened. One by one the others begin to rise and shine. Your roommate seems totally unaware that anything out of the ordinary occurred. So does his boyfriend. What do you do or say?

GAY QUESTIONS

220

You're dating Rafael, a man whose company you really enjoy. You're shocked when a neighbor who sees the two of you together calls and urges you to be careful. The neighbor refuses to be specific but insists that Rafael is "trouble with a capital T." Would you heed his advice? Would you discuss the conversation with Rafael? If so, what would you say?

GAY QUESTIONS

221

Your doctor prescribes a new medication for a chronic health problem. He explains that it's superior to the drug you've been taking but warns that impotence is a possible side effect. Would you take it?

222

A friend of yours constantly operates on "gay time," and you've grown tired of constantly waiting for him. Do you confront him, withdraw from the friendship, or deal with it by always telling him to meet you a half hour earlier than you intend to be there?

GAY QUESTIONS

223

Your friend is an administrator for a prominent cosmetic surgeon and can arrange for you to have any procedure performed free of charge. What, if anything, would you have done?

224

Which do you think America is most likely to experience first—a female president, an African-American president, or an openly gay president? Do you think this will occur during your lifetime?

GAY QUESTIONS

225

You work in the records department of a major hospital. An international superstar has been secretly admitted under an assumed name. The mission? A penile enlargement. You have access to documentation. You also have a stack of personal bills that could be paid in full with the money the *National Enquirer* would surely pay for your hot tip. Do you call them with the scoop? If not, would your decision be different if your anonymity were guaranteed?

GAY QUESTIONS

226

A respected television news program is producing a one-hour special on "Gays in America." The show will profile six gay men and lesbians. One of the producers was given your name by a friend of a friend and is interested in sending a camera crew to spend several days documenting your life. Would you agree to participate? If not, why?

GAY QUESTIONS

227

Have you ever intentionally given another man a wrong phone number? Why?

228

How many of your friends would you be willing to let move in to your home for a month or two? Name them.

GAY QUESTIONS

229

Is honesty always the best policy? You're on a weekend trip with a longtime friend and are getting ready for a night on the town. When he emerges from the bathroom, you can't help noticing that his clothes not only are two sizes too small but also look like they were borrowed from his 13-year-old son's closet. You know your 40-something friend is sensitive about aging but have never seen him exhibit his insecurity quite so blatantly. When he asks, "So how do I look?" do you tell him the truth?

GAY QUESTIONS

230

How many times a day would you say you think about sex? Do you think that's more often or less often than other men your age?

231

"Morality," Oscar Wilde once observed, "is simply the attitude we adopt toward people whom we personally dislike." Whom or what do you consider immoral? Would you say you're more or less easily offended than most people you know?

GAY QUESTIONS

232

Is there anything too serious or too sacred to be joked about? What?

233

What do you know about yourself today that you wish you'd known five years ago?

GAY QUESTIONS

234

Sex researcher Alfred Kinsey once remarked that "the only unnatural sex act is that which you cannot perform." What, if anything, do you find "unnatural"?

235

If you discovered you had only two weeks to live, how would you live them? Whom would you spend the time with? What, if any, unfinished business would you feel compelled to resolve?

GAY QUESTIONS

236

You're out to your immediate family, and over time they've become politely supportive. Your elderly aunt Alice is visiting from out of town and over a family dinner asks you when you're going to find the right girl and settle down. How do you respond?

237

What's the one thing you'd be most embarrassed to have people know about you?

GAY QUESTIONS

238

When the hunk you've been dating shows up one night after shaving off his mustache, it's all too apparent why he grew one in the first place. He's obviously pleased with his new look. You are not. What, if anything, do you say?

239

Which do you trust more—your intuition or your intelligence?

GAY QUESTIONS

240

Ambrose Bierce once defined a bore as "a person who talks when you wish him to listen." Who's the biggest bore you know? When's the last time you were a bore? Did you realize it at the time?

241

If you could be 20 years old again, would you do it? Under what conditions? If so, how would you live life differently the second time around?